SOUL FREEDOM

My Journey to Finding Unconditional Love

DEBRA ENILE ARMAND

ISBN: 979-8-9881440-0-7

Published by:
RedTrini Publishing

Cover design by:
Rehmanx_x

Edited by:
Spirit of Excellence Writing & Editing Services, LLC
www.TakeUpThySword.com

Acknowledgements

I would not be where I am today without the unconditional love of God, my two sons Jonathan and Joshua Armand (their future wives, their children, grandchildren, and great-grandchildren, for this is also part of their legacy), and the numerous people I have had the pleasure to encounter who have shown me love in one form or another (the best way they knew how). To the numerous teachers and lessons learned through life experiences, who have taught me how to embrace painful lessons and use them to make me better and not bitter, I am forever grateful. To all my spiritual teachers along the way who have helped me to build upon a solid biblical foundation, I thank you.

I am not a licensed therapist nor a great spiritual teacher. I am a woman who has stubbornly refused to settle for the status quo when I know deep within me that there is more, abundantly more, than I can ever think or imagine about this thing called unconditional love. What qualifies me to write on this topic is my relentless search, a yearning that would not be satisfied by a counterfeit form, my experiences and a God who continues to relentlessly pursue me and has commissioned me to write about what I have learned so far. It is a journey that continues and I pray it will be a help to you along your journey.

If I could speak all the languages on earth and of angels (be highly educated and intelligent) but did not (unconditionally) love others, I would only be a noisy gong or a clanging cymbal. If I had the gift of prophecy and if I understood all of God's secret plans and possessed all knowledge, and if I had faith that I could move mountains (be highly spiritual) but did not (unconditionally) love others, I would be nothing. If I gave everything I have to the poor and even sacrificed my body (as a martyr) to be burnt but I did not (unconditionally) love others, I would gain nothing. 1 Corinthians 13:1-3 (Amplified version paraphrased).

Table of Contents

Introduction

What is love? If you ask anyone what the definition of love is, you will get as many varied responses as there are people on the earth. Most of us define love by what we have been shown, what we experienced in our early childhood, or by our deep inner longings of what we most desire. Some of us get our definition from romantic books, movies, or the media. I will attempt to unfold aspects of the true meaning of love as we go along in this book.

I would dare add that all we have learned and the information and experiences we have gathered so far in our lives is only the tip of the iceberg of the vastness of true love. I believe it is greater than anything our minds or hearts can imagine or conceive.

Unconditional love is the root of the tree that brings forth the fruits of patience, kindness, inner peace, joy, humility, unselfishness, self-control, faithfulness, self-control, faithfulness, goodness, compassion, forgiveness and so on. It is the foundation for building a successful life within oneself and with the relationships outside of ourselves. It is like building a house. In Matthew 7:24-27, Jesus taught us, saying:

> So, everyone who hears these words of Mine and acts on them, will be like a wise man (a far-sighted, practical, and sensible man) who built his house on the Rock. And the rain fell, and the floods and torrents came, and the winds blew and slammed against that house; yet it did not fall, because it had been founded on the Rock. And everyone who hears these words of Mine and does not do them, will be like a foolish (stupid) man who built his house on the sand. And the rain fell, and the floods and torrents came, and the winds blew and slammed against that house; and it fell – and great and complete was its fall.

Every house that will stand through the adversities of the ages must be built on a solid foundation, the Rock, which I will refer to here as unconditional love. It will withstand the storms and torrents of life. Love is what we need and want within ourselves and others in order to cohabitate on this earth peacefully and happily. I believe that deep within every human being is the desire to be unconditionally loved and accepted, and there is joy in this journey.

Chapter 1
In the Beginning
What unconditional love is not

To write about my present journey, I must revisit my past and go back to the beginning of my first memory, impression, and teaching of what I learned about what love is or is not.

The first childhood memory I have, is of a 4-year-old me, standing outside of our home in the scorching sun, half-naked, crying as my mother and eldest sister tried to rescue me and bring me indoors; but my father was blocking their way saying, "No, leave her outside in the sun until she gets black" (dark-skinned like my other siblings). Years later, I asked my mom's only living sibling (my aunt) if this was a true recollection of that event or did I imagine this. She affirmed that this took place. Much later in life after failed relationships and an insatiable desire for inner healing, I discovered that this event was the catalyst, the seed planted in a 4-year-old's heart, that translated to her a message that she was not good enough to be loved, that something was wrong with her, and she was unlovable just the way she was. This message given to her by the first man in her life, her earthly father, who was given the divine duty to teach her what love was.

All my tumultuous life with my dad, I heard it said that he did not consider me his child. I heard adult family members whisper about it, some of my siblings verbally attacked me with these words, and I saw the rejection in my father's eyes when he looked at me. This was all because the color of my skin was fairer in complexion than the rest of my 4 darker-skinned siblings. You see, my dad was very dark-skinned and my mom was very fair. Being uneducated and ignorant (I say that respectfully) of the fact that one can produce children with both familial traits, my father held me as an outcast, the "black" sheep of the family.

As an innocent child, I could not understand what I did wrong. I could not understand why he could not love me. Children do that - they take the blame of an adult's dysfunction upon themselves. They internalize it, make it their own and carry that within them, sometimes for the rest of their lives. Those planted seeds became the breeding ground for insecurities, feelings of low self-worth, and victimhood. And the thing about seeds is that they grow. Their roots went deep within my soul as I unconsciously looked at every relationship to find evidence of what I believed about myself. I often tell my adult children, that people cannot make you feel anything about yourself, that you do not already believe.

As the seeds grew, they manifested in fear of vulnerability masked as anger, living defensively in a world I felt was unsafe, and rebellion along with a passionate need to succeed and prove my father wrong, to make him see that I was (I am) "somebody." I could be loved. It was almost schizophrenic, rebelling to get attention, while trying to get his love that my soul so desperately craved. But with my relationships, if anything came close to looking like "love," I would (unconsciously) do whatever I could to push it away (self-sabotage) because of this deep-rooted belief of unworthiness, which also affected the way I viewed God the Father, God the Son and God the Holy Spirit. I will get into that later.

Chapter 2
Daddy's Little Girl

The role of a father is so important in establishing how a child views love and therefore, the world around them. But fathers cannot give what they have never been given or never been shown. When they have never been shown or received true love, they are unable to pass that on to their children.

My dad's story

I did not come to know much about my father's upbringing until years after his death. As an adult, I learned that my dad had a very traumatic childhood. He was homeless as a teenager, cast out of his home by his mother, and periodically being taken in and cared for by various relatives - particularly one sister who cared for him until she migrated to the United States. He then went to live with an uncle in the capital city of Port-of-Spain, Trinidad, who was a baker and taught him the trade. He was again cast out when he accidentally dropped a glass jar into the dough mixer, thus ruining the entire batch. He later lived in the same area where he met and married my mother.

My father was a tormented soul, which manifested in his womanizing and physically abusing my mother. I saw things as a child that no child should see. It was a volatile household, yet because of the lack of his education, he was fastidious about his children's. I learned that this was one area where I could please my dad and get some semblance of acceptance from him, so I tried my best to excel in school. I did not learn until I was a teenager that my dad could not read until I saw him reading the newspaper upside down. My mom did everything for him that required any reading or writing. Dad was a hard worker, who sacrificed to provide and care for his household. I appreciated that about him.

A child is born and needs love and acceptance from its parents/caregivers. I am told that the healthy emotional connection between a child and its father is paramount in formulating future healthy emotional relationships, and I would dare say that includes a spiritual relationship with God. Every child (no matter the circumstances that brought them into this world), needs and deserves love. Because most of us were raised by caregivers who did not receive such love (no judgement here), it resulted in an emotional deficit that not only affected our lives but also those connected to us in our homes, at our jobs, or in the world we interact with daily. The deficits (sins) of the father/parent are passed down to their children.

It was not until I was in my mid-fifties, comprehending the unconditional love of God in more depth, that I finally began to take care for myself, my body (physically) and my mind (emotionally). This all stemmed from my unconscious core beliefs I had about myself that were developed in my early childhood relationships. The emotional deficits manifested in my physical well-being. I ate whatever foods I wanted regardless of the negative effects they had on my body. There were times I used food to soothe my emotional pain and as a protective device from being attractive to the opposite sex; I thought to myself, there would be no rejection and I could control who I let in that would not hurt me. This gave some sense of temporary pleasure but had long-term consequences of type 2 diabetes, high blood pressure, and high cholesterol levels (the Troublesome Trio, I call them), which are precursors for heart/kidney disease and other medical ailments.

Eating junk food will never lead to a healthy life, just as eating emotional junk food will never cure the deep pain and unhealed wounds within. It only keeps us emotionally unhealthy like being on a hamster wheel and wanting desperately to get off because we know that life can be better than the way we are living. The unhealthy emotional junk we use (sex, power, relationships, drugs, shopping, etc.) will only bring a temporary relief, a false sense of safety/control, but it does not heal the deep pain within.

In my case, I got some temporary relief from my father's disdain for me by receiving his praise when I got good grades in school. But I still saw the difference in his response to me. When my siblings presented their great report cards (only A's and Bs were acceptable), my dad's face would light up with a magnanimous smile, displaying his pearly white teeth set against the bluish black of his skin. I longed to also receive that genuine smile of approval, so I studied hard and tried to bring home only A's or place first in my elementary classes. I would see my mom giving him my report cards and I believe she too held out hope of some display of his love and approval towards me. But no matter how I search through my memories, I cannot recall seeing the brightness of his smile, twinkle of love in his eyes, or words of approval for my achievements. Instead, I would receive a nonchalant look or a nod. As children do, I kept trying (and some adults are still trying) to get those words of love, affirmation, and acceptance from parents who were incapable of doing so.

All we have ever wanted and needed was true love and acceptance for our successes, failures, or efforts, of just being us. I believe so many have difficulty in being their true selves because they have had to be chameleons to receive love and acceptance from those who mattered most in their lives. For some, it is so difficult to even know who they truly are, walking through life with false identities and interchangeable face masks just to be accepted.

Chapter 3
What Is Love?

The question is not so much what is love, because love is a WHO. So, WHO is love?

First John 4:8 and 4:16 says that God is love. It is not part of His character and it is not what He does. Love is WHO He is. God is the definition of love. God is also eternal, so that means love existed before you or I ever did. Before the formation of the earth or the galaxies, there was God, so there was love. God is also infinite, so my finite mind cannot fully comprehend the vastness of who God is or the extent of His love.

First Corinthians 13:13 talks about faith, hope and love. When did faith appear? What is necessary for faith and hope to exist? Is it predicated on human connections? Faith is powerful - it can move mountains and it is necessary for living a successful, purpose-driven life. Hope is also essential because we may faint, give up, or end our lives without hope. These three most powerful spiritual principles, are as necessary to the human experience as the air we breathe. Yet the Bible tells us that of these three most powerful spiritual forces on the earth, the greatest of these is love because love existed before faith and hope and will continue for eternity when our faith is realized as we see Jesus's face to face one day in heaven. Our hope in Christ will come to an end when we arrive in heaven because it is only necessary for our earthly existence. But love, love will go on forever, because God is love and we will be with love throughout all eternity.

Love is God. He is the source of true unconditional love. In order to charge your cell phone, you must have an electrical outlet source. We have been looking for love yet keep plugging into the wrong sources. No wonder we are still left feeling unfulfilled. Is sex the source of love? Is alcohol or drugs the source of love? Is your husband, wife, boyfriend, or girlfriend the source of love? Is it your children, education, the job, external validation from the people around you, traveling the globe, or partying? What have you been using as the source of your emotional healing? There is only one remedy to heal the hurts, the childhood traumas, and the life scars and that is unconditional love; and the source for that is God.

Without fully comprehending this truth earlier on in my life, the search continued for me in finding love and I looked in all the wrong places and in all the wrong faces. The obvious choice as a teenage girl, was to engage in a relationship with a boy, yearning to be unconditionally loved and this started very early in my life at the age of fifteen. Having a boyfriend, I unconsciously hoped that he would fill this love void deep within my soul. There was an unspoken expectation that, as women in my Caribbean culture, our goal in life was to do well educationally, get married and raise a family. There is nothing wrong with that, but I was not taught on an emotional level, as to the source of love and how to plug into that source. My parents did not know so they could not give what they did not have, and they did the best they could with what they knew.

I was introduced to church at an early age. I went to Catholic school and evangelical vacation Bible school but only emerged seeing God as a stern disciplinarian who allowed His Son Jesus Christ to suffer on a cross. We were taught about the punishment for sin and the fire and brimstone of hell (we were taught more about hell than about heaven), but very few of the Bible teachers I had expounded on the love of God. Looking back, I believe that they did not know about the unfathomable love of God in a deep, nourishing, emotionally healing way. Since my earthly father was a stern disciplinarian and that was the only father figure I knew, I related to God from that place of woundedness, that place of never feeling good enough for the Christian life and never feeling worthy enough of God's love. I only saw God as a stern father. So, I unconsciously searched and longed for the one that would unconditionally love and accept me for who I was.

Chapter 4
The Road Much Traveled

Searching for someone I could feel safe with led to paths taken where I learned what love was not. My emotional insecurities and feelings of low self-worth led me to make poor choices in partners. At the age of 15, I was still a virgin in high school. My group of friends had already lost their virginity and expounded on their sexual conquests or adventures. Wanting to be a "girl of the world", to fit in, to be like my friends, I decided I needed to lose my virginity also. Being insecure and wanting to feel some form of love and be accepted by my small clique of girlfriends that I had somehow became the leader of. How can I be the biggest mouth in the group, the leader of the group, and still be a virgin? They would think I was a fraud if they only knew the truth. So, this was my impetus in deciding to give up my virginity at the age of 15, to be accepted by my friends. On the other side of the coin of keeping my chastity intact, was a deep fear of my father if I became a teenage mother like my older siblings and honestly, I did not want to be one. I always wanted more out of life. And that kept me a virgin till then.

So poor decision number 1 was made. Poor decision number 2 was the mistake of giving this precious gift to a young man we call in my culture, "the village ram goat." He was the one who slept with as many girls as possible. He was tall, very good-looking, and very desired among the teenage girls. "Johnny with the good hair" will be my nickname for him. I was just a conquest for him, a notch in his belt, to boast about with his cronies. It was a horrible experience; there was nothing loving about it as I imagined it would be. I knew this was not love, at least not the love I wanted. So even though I could now contribute to the conversations with my high school friends, I still did not feel loved. As with many, sex is equated to love, so women/girls give up their bodies in hopes of getting a man to love them. That experience of losing my virginity in such a foolish manner made me withhold myself emotionally from future suitors.

When I did decide to have a boyfriend again at the end of high school and the beginning of my nursing college years, I always wanted to be sure that they loved me more than I thought I loved them. You see, by this time, I lived in survival mode by controlling relationships, people, and situations due to the fear of being hurt. I felt that if I controlled the outcome, I would be safe and people would not reject me like my dad did. Looking back in hindsight, I did not know this was what I was doing or why I was making those choices at the time. But no matter what love or loyalty was expressed or given to me, there was a bridge I would not let myself cross to become completely open, vulnerable, and receptive to their adoration because I did not know how to love them back. I knew love was not sex but I never truly felt deeply emotionally connected to these partners.

Then one day at the tender age of 18, I met someone and something happened deep within me that was difficult to describe and took 40 years to figure out. I met a young medical intern. There was something about this young man that made me feel connected to him and safe in some way. I have a vivid memory of watching him walk across our hospital compound. I was standing in the medicine room above, looking out the window, staring at him while forgetting the pain medication I came to retrieve for my hurting patient. I remember looking at him until he disappeared under the walkway of the first-floor building of the hospital. When I met him, I did not know at that time that I would never truly want to give my heart to anyone else, at least not completely.

We dated for a brief time but this did not end in a fairy tale. We married different people, had kids, and lived different lives in different parts of the globe. But deep inside me for a very long time, I always wanted to be with him. Many times, I tried to let it go but I had built up this fairytale story in my head of what my life would be like with him: he would protect me, he would be my safe place and he would love me the way I longed to be loved. That was the story I made up and kept in my head for 40 years. And I thought this feeling I had must be love, right?

At the tender age of 23 after migrating to the United States, I met my first husband, the father of my two wonderful sons, and remained married for 20 years. I realized later in life that this marriage was about me wanting acceptance. As a young nurse from the Caribbean islands of Trinidad and Tobago with no close family members nearby, I wanted to be accepted into a family. I was still not accepted into his and it took a very long time for me to release that rejection. But we both had emotional issues and we thought being Christians and being faithful in the church would fix it.

Do not get me wrong, becoming a Christian and learning about Christ was the best decision I've ever made in my life. It helped but deep down inside, there were still broken areas that kept us repeating unhealthy patterns over and over and over again. God has created us with different components that we are responsible for: the spiritual, the emotional, the physical, and the mental aspects of our being. I believe as Christians, we focus most of our resources on the spiritual but neglect the other aspects of our true selves (neglect might be an incorrect term but it is the only thing I can think of at this time). I believe we are not knowledgeable about how our emotional childhood traumas affect the rest of our relationships.

When my first marriage ended, I quickly rebelled against God and married what I now call "my fears and insecurities," which was my second husband. Yes, he had a name but the true reason I married him was because of my own unhealed emotional wounds. He also had his own emotional demons that he did not know how to deal with and even after being offered the resources for emotional healing, he chose not to pursue it. Out of that marriage and divorce would come my biggest blessing: the gift of beginning this journey to my own emotional healing.

Fake love

You may ask yourself; how can I tell if someone truly loves me or not? Have you ever seen the *Catfish* TV shows or the Netflix documentary called *The Tinder Swindler*. Have you ever listened to life coaches or counselors or read about how to spot the red flags of an emotional abuser? They are crafty and skillful manipulators who prey on the vulnerabilities of emotionally unhealthy individuals. My advice on this is not to concentrate on spotting the fake love but to educate yourself on what true unconditional love is. I have heard stories that banks train their employees to identify what authentic dollar bills look like, and they become so proficient that they can easily detect the fake bills because they know what the real ones look like. I believe it is the same when looking for authentic love. Learn what true unconditional love is and you will not be deceived or misguided by the fake love that disguises itself as the genuine thing.

Chapter 5
The Source of My Unconditional Love

Because of my faith in Christ Jesus, I will share these few scriptures that have been impactful in my life and in my journey as I attempted to comprehend this unexplainable, undeniable, inexhaustible, limitless love of God that I do not fully grasp, nor can fully explain with my finite abilities. The journeys to discovering Who love is has been life-changing, life-altering, adventurous, amazing, frightening and sometimes totally awe-inspiring.

I will attempt to do this in my own words, making it as simple as possible and not a theological dissertation. Romans 5:8 says that God demonstrated His own unconditional love for us in that while we were yet sinners, still living in sin, Christ died for us. Why is this important? It takes me to another scripture in 1 John 4:10 that says this is unconditional love: not that we loved God but that He unconditionally loved us and sent His Son, His only begotten Son, as an atoning sacrifice for your sins and mine. What does the word atone mean? It's defined as making amends for a wrong one has done or helping those who have been wronged. Jesus repaired the original sin in the garden of Eden made by Adam and Eve.

So, this is where I started on this journey, realizing I knew deep within me that God loved me even though I felt unworthy of that love. I knew I was taught that and I thought I believed that fully, but sometimes you must stop and think about what this means. What this meant for me was that while I was out looking for love in all the wrong places and faces, God unconditionally loved me. When my earthly father rejected me as his own (because he knew no better and never received nor knew how to give unconditional love), God loved me unconditionally. And He loved me so much that He made a way to atone for my sins so I could be with Him throughout all eternity.

The Father did not wave a magic wand and He did not take away my will to choose, which to me is the highest form of love: free will. God took on the form of human flesh in the form of his Son Jesus Christ, who willingly came to this earth, suffered, bled, and died a horrible death to atone for my sins (to be my sin-sacrifice), because He loved me that much. I know this: unconditional love gives, it is not about taking from others. Love is not selfish and love is not about what we can get but what we have within us to give to those in our lives and those we encounter, without expecting anything in return. Zephaniah 3:17 says that the Lord your God is with you, Immanuel, the Mighty warrior who saves. He will take great delight in you, in His love, He will no longer rebuke you, but He will rejoice over you with singing.

So many may ask (like I have asked before): God, if you loved me so much why did you allow me to go through those hurtful things as a child? Why did you place me in that family? Why couldn't I have been born into a loving family? Then I go back to this verse in Zephaniah that God is Immanuel - He is with us. He has never left my side; through every trial and every test that has shaped my character up to this point, God has been with me. God has used all my experiences to bring me to a place of surrender, to become a broken, beautiful, cherished vessel of His, so I can share with others that unconditional love is here to receive, to embrace to embody. So, He's never left my side not once, and I believe what He told me in His Word that He never will.

First John 3:1 (NIV) says, "See what great love the Father has lavished on us, that we [you and I] should be called children of God!" For everyone who has felt like an orphan, for everyone who has been rejected by their parents (in one form or another), given up by caregivers. For everyone who has been ignored, overlooked, not fully seen, or accepted by those who were entrusted to love and care for them. For everyone who lost parents, and regardless of what circumstances brought you into this world, we are still children of God and He wants to lavish His love on us. And that is who we are! This is where I get my source of love - this is my emotional socket and my power source.

The world does not know what true love is because the world does not know or want to know the source of love, or it has rejected the Source. Take an inventory of the different things, places, people, or even animals that we look to as the source. Is it a person you are looking towards? What if they have never received true love and don't even know what it looks like and how to give it? Is it a job, the power of accomplishments, or the praise of men that you think will make you feel love and acceptance? Most of us know that is a fleeting experience. Have you ever heard the phrase, "today a hero, tomorrow a zero"? Are you an animal lover like I am and think you will get unconditional love from your pet? Where is your source of love coming from? What are you plugged into?

First John 4:7 (NIV) says, "Dear friends, let us love one another, for love comes from God. Everyone who loves [unconditionally] has been born of God and knows God." So how can we love if we are not plugged into the right source? We cannot, and we will keep searching or continuing to live relatively empty, emotional lives while trying to fill it with joyful pleasurable distractions. I must stay plugged into my spiritual source because I do not know what love is without Him and it's difficult to love unconditionally in my own strength. We must be connected spiritually (to the right source) to grow emotionally, which will manifest physically.

First John 4:16 (NIV) says, "And so we know and rely on the love God has for us. God is love. Whoever lives in love lives in God, and God in them." That is where my love comes from inside of me to give to those outside of me. God in me makes my nature unconditionally loving because God is love. Right here, I want to say, Selah: stop, pause, think, and meditate on what I just said. I have tried loving before but it has always been conditional. This is the way I have been wired from childhood. Due to the emotional trauma and misguidance by my caretakers, love was always given and taught on a conditional basis (which is the same for most, if not all, human beings). For example, if you excel in academia, sports or other talents, then you will be shown love. Some of us have learned that praise is equated with love. When we behave well, we do the right things, and we are well-mannered (which is all good), most of it is to make our parents, guardians or caretakers look good in the eyes of their friends, relatives, or neighbors. And when we do that, we get praise and therefore learn that love is conditional. It always reflects to "What's in it for me?" And that is a sobering reality.

First John 4:19 (NIV) says, "We love because He first loved us." This is powerful, so let us break it down. The question here is: how do we know what love is and what does that look like? Some, if not most of us, can spend a lifetime searching for it, substituting for it, compromising for it, or trying to define it but will never recognize or pursue true unconditional love until we encounter and accept God's love for us. He is the author, the originator, and the nature of love. If you are searching for love, why not start here?

Stop plugging into imitations, artificial, bogus, false, and synthetic sources that only give temporary pleasure or temporary relief from your inner emotional pain. Unconditional love heals. And

I have learned this: the more I heal, the less I hurt. Why keep repeating the same patterns of dysfunctional behavior and accepting or being attracted to the same type of dysfunctional people? Why continue living this way when God has offered us free access into the most powerful spiritual, emotional, and intellectual source on the face of this planet? What is the alternative? For me, the opposite of love is fear and that is the state I lived in most of my life.

Chapter 6
Fear Is a Brutal Master

When we have never been given or taught or experienced love, we grow up in systems based on lies or untruths about who we are as a person (our identity), what our worth and value is, what we can become or who we are destined to be. We innocently believed those initial lies from loved ones who unknowingly taught us that we were unworthy beings, of little or no value, or only worthy of love based on what we could give to them. Because they grew up with the same untruths about their own worth and value, this creates the perfect storm of fear and dysfunction. When this is all we know, it becomes normal for us. Chaos becomes normal, survivable comfort zones.

Well, the truth is you and I were created with great worth and value. In Jeremiah 1:5, God says, "Before I formed you in the womb, I knew you and approved of you as My chosen instrument." One of the most profound truths in my life is found in Psalm 139:16 that says, "Your eyes have seen my unformed substance; And in Your book were all written the days that were appointed for me, when as yet there was not one of them even taking shape." Another truth that is profound in my life is found in verse 14 of that same chapter: "I will give thanks and praise to You for I am fearfully and wonderfully made." Let that sink in for a bit, then mediate on these truths of how valuable you are - another Selah moment.

There are a ton of truths in the Word of God that tells us about our worth, our value, our purpose, and our destiny. My foundational truth is found in Jeremiah 29:11 (NIV): "'For I know the plans I have for you,' declares the Lord, 'plans to prosper you and not to harm you, plans to give you hope and a future.'" Very early in my Christian walk, I found this scripture and I believed this, and I have stood upon this scripture most of my life.

Fear cripples everything good we can believe about ourselves. It directs our thoughts to everything negative that is filled with doubt and unbelief. Our thoughts form our emotions, our emotions form our actions and decisions, and our actions determine our lifestyle and the outcome of our lives. Fear is the perfect recipe to live a self-defeating life. It does not matter if you were born in a palace or in the ghetto, fear torments and destroys dreams and any potential within us. It wreaks havoc and brings unrest; it robs us of peace. Our minds are constantly tortured but the good news is that there is hope and freedom and it is found in love - God's unconditional love. First John 4:18 is another one of my favorite truths and it says, "There is no fear in love (dread does not exist). But perfect (complete, full grown) love drives out fear."

Now there is a fear of God, not a dreadful fear but a reverential fear. It is not the fear that makes you hide from Him like Adam and Eve did in the garden after they had sinned. For much of my life, I did not fully comprehend what God's love was about. I measured His love by the conditional love I was taught in my childhood. I thought that if I performed well, He would reward me and return His love and affection to me (this is transactional, not unconditional). Growing up only hearing fire and brimstone sermons surely did not help me to see God as a loving Father but only as one who waited to punish me for the smallest infraction. This instilled an unhealthy fear of God that unconsciously continued throughout most of my early adulthood. Where there is dreaded fear, there will be distrust. The more I learned about the true character of God and what love truly is, 1 John 4:18 not only made sense but it became the nature of the type of love I sought to receive and to give.

I could now trust that Jeremiah 29:11 was not only my promise, but it became my process. I came to believe God's Word had been preparing me for my earthly purpose, my destiny. I came to trust and believe that God knew the path that I should take and like others before me, He would not hurt me in the process. I began to truly learn how to love Him unconditionally, which resulted in the truth that if I could love Him, then I could trust Him. And if I trusted Him, I could obey His commandments, His Word, His way, and His path; it became an exhilarating journey. The more I learned about the character of God and what love truly is, I began to love myself because I began to see myself the way He sees me. I am thankful for the journey and the life experiences (some very painful) that taught me what love was not. Those painful experiences lit more fire in my soul to hunger and thirst for true love.

God's unconditional love not only changed my heart, it changed the way I view the world and the people in my world. It also changed the way I pray. Reexamining my prayer life, I saw much of my prayers were fear-based, anxiety-filled requests begging God for my will to be done rather than praying in faith, which was based in trusting Him for His will and being patient while trusting Him.

Trusting Him that solutions were coming because He unconditionally loved me. This one was a game changer for me, releasing fear and choosing to live with unconditional love.

Chapter 7
The Mind Regulator

As I sat in church one day, I heard this terminology again about Jesus being a mind regulator. I had heard the elders in church many times over the years describe mind regulation as one of the characteristics of God. In my early Christian years, I took this to mean that He can keep me from literally going crazy as I dealt with the emotional pain of a failed marriage. Believe me, there were times when I thought that I would lose my mind; the emotional pain was that intense. I listened to the testimonies of other believers through the years who confessed that if it had not been for the Lord, they would have lost their minds. Many songs have also been written about this topic. For this season of my journey, to me, it meant God wants to change me by changing the way I think.

After my second divorce, I found myself attracted to this man I met on an online dating site and we began to talk outside of the app. This is where I became very cognizant of my anxious attachment style and why this contributed to past failed relationships. I also learned that this attachment style was part of my codependent nature because of my own unhealed childhood emotional trauma. This type of attachment is all fear-based. I attached to people quickly out of fear of losing them, fear of being alone, fear that I was not good enough, and feelings of unworthiness that had nothing to do with the other person.

This fear of not getting what I desired from a life partner was ingrained in me as a child. Fear created anxiety and questions such as: will they call, will they text, when will they call, when will they text back, will we ever meet, what if it does not work out, what if he does not

like me when he sees me, what if...what if....what if.... All creating more anxiety and coming from past hurts being projected into the present and forecasting a negative future and a negative present-day mindset.

I was on a short solo road trip when all the previous information came flooding in and it scared me. There is that fear again. I saw the real problem: it was my mind, the way my mindset was developed for self-protection by placing walls around myself because of fear of being hurt. It was a mindset of survival, and I knew I no longer wanted to live this way. I wanted and needed to be free. I wanted a new way of thinking and a new way of being. I needed the mind regulator. So, with the open freeway before me as I drove, I literally cried out to God. I needed His help.

I would obey what He had already shown me (years ago) on this journey of learning about unconditional love, I would trade my fears, mainly based on all those inherited lies, for His truth. In the areas of my life such as my feelings of low self-worth and need for external validation to feel good about myself was where I would begin to do the work. I knew what I had to do when I got home. I was tired of swiping right or left or connecting with men who needed to do their own emotional work. I committed to educating myself about becoming free from this anxious attachment style; the deeper inner work had continued on a deeper level. The road to freedom is like peeling back an onion, layer by layer, and I knew that God's Holy Spirit was right there with me.

Chapter 8
Sorting Through

Now at the young age of 57, I found myself single and back in the dating pool. It was a different world from when I last dated 34 years prior. I found myself doing online dating because that is how you meet most people today, but I was not enjoying the experience. I found a lot of catfish scammers and learned how to filet fish. I found that most men in my age group were looking for younger versions of what they previously had. And I got tons of likes from younger men who were probably interested in forming relationships to find a "sugar mama." I got a lot of interest from men but I was mainly interested in those who lived miles from my hometown; distance was safety for me I later realized. Then my younger son said, "Mom, you're not ready to date."

So, I took more time to sort through my inner emotions and continue doing the inner healing work to identify and resolve emotional areas that still need to be healed. This has brought me to Romans 12:1-2, that says "Therefore I urge you, brothers, and sisters, by the mercies of God, to present your bodies (dedicating all of yourselves, set apart) as a living sacrifice, holy and well-pleasing to God, which is your rational (logical, intelligent) act of worship. And do not be conformed to this world (any longer with its superficial values and customs), but be transformed and progressively changed (as you mature spiritually) by the renewing of your mind (focusing on godly values and ethical attitudes), so that you may prove (for yourselves) what the will of God is, that which is good and acceptable and perfect (in His plan and purpose for you)." This passage of scripture helped me to see that my discouraging thoughts about online dating or dating in general were creating emotions about how I was thinking about myself and my situation. This is one of the keys for my emotional healing and growth: identifying and addressing what is going on within rather than believing or relying on outside influences to fix an inner problem. The issue was not what was happening on the dating apps but how I was allowing this process to reveal how I felt about myself while realizing that I still had some more inner healing work to do.

I had to get brutally honest with myself. I was feeling unworthy and lonely. I wanted human companionship, and meaningful conversations with the opposite sex. I think of Genesis chapter 1 where God said that it is not good for man (or humankind) to be alone. So, we all long for human connection and unconditional love. I accepted that and I wanted that at that time.

So now back to Romans 12:1-2. The first verse, was voluntarily surrendering my body, including my mind, my thoughts, and my emotions, as a living sacrifice to God. My Christian journey thus far had led me to believe that if I did this, the Holy Spirit would fill me so much that I would have no need or desire for a relationship; and by surrendering completely to God, I would be completely healed inside and not carry the hurts of my past. This is true to a certain point but it is also a process, and the first step is surrendering my thoughts, my mind, the thinking that was formulated in childhood of who I was or what I told myself about who I am and what I became to believe of who I was.

A good exercise would be to take some time and listen to what you are telling yourself about yourself. God tells me that I will be transformed into the person He created me to be by the renewing of my mind and my thought patterns that created my belief system that generated my emotions. So, I began to sort through my thoughts to discard the lies and replace them with the truth. Tell yourself the truth. Before we can be truthful with others, we first must be truthful to ourselves. One of my lies was that I was unworthy of attracting a man with the qualities I desired. My lie was that the good ones were probably all taken, or there were very few left who were honest believers.

My truth was that I was feeling lonely for male companionship and I must learn to navigate this new dating world while remaining pure and true to God and myself. So, I began to replace the lies with the truth. As Jeremiah 29:11 reminds me, God has a great plan for me. He had a great future already prepared for me and I knew that my alone time with Him did not have to be a lonely time. It was a time God was using to heal my emotional wounds, preparing me for the future He had for me. So that meant that He was also preparing someone for me.

I no longer had to conform to the world standards, games, or manipulations in order to get a partner. Be careful of decisions you make in your alone times. Do not allow them to become lonely times, because the best decisions are not made when you are lonely. I began to use my thirsty times for male companionship to be thirsty times for God's presence. Instead of the dating app, which I deleted, I delved more into the Bible app so I could renew my mind. I am fearfully and wonderfully made, created by the Master of the universe, and God's Word was stored up within my heart and mind, to share with the partner He was preparing for me and the world.

So yes, I am worthy of God's unconditional love. His Agape love. He said so in John 3:16. He showed me that I am worthy of His love by sending His only Son to die for my sins so I can spend eternity with Him. I can love God unconditionally; I am still learning. It is a journey but my heart's desire is to love Him with all my mind, heart, and soul and to love myself so I can love my neighbor and my life partner as I love myself. My emotions are changing with these truths and the future is looking much brighter.

Conclusion

Lately I have been singing the song, "What the World Needs Now Is Love Sweet Love." We see it every day through road rage incidents that are sometimes fatal; people losing control at airports, restaurants, hospitals, or home; our political systems; and the way we treat each other... all because of a lack of genuine love in the world. It reminds me of the Bible truth in Mathew 24:12 that says, "Because lawlessness is increased, the love of most people will grow cold." This is in reference to how the world will be before Jesus Christ returns. God is still working in us to shine His love in our hearts and lives so we can live an abundant life and be able to give this love to others.

As I have said, this is an ongoing journey - my journey that has given me freedom. My perspectives have changed spiritually, emotionally, physically, and intellectually. Because of this inner healing journey, I have changed the way I eat and have lost 49 pounds so far. I joined the gym and began exercising, not to look good but to take care of this one body that God has given me responsibility for. The outward results are due to the inner work. I create great recipes that are beneficial for the healing of my body. My mind is being renewed daily.

Third John 1:2 says, "Beloved, I pray that in every way you may succeed and prosper and be in good health (physically), just as (I know) your soul prospers (spiritually and emotionally)." Your soul becomes free when your perspectives change and you can know and understand that all things and all circumstances will help you grow spiritually and heal emotionally when you trust that everything God does for you comes from a place of unconditional love. That is soul freedom.